D0433735

DESPICABLE ME 3: COMPLETE GUIDE TO GADGETS AND VEHICLES

A CENTUM BOOK 9781911460404

PUBLISHED IN GREAT BRITAIN BY CENTUM BOOKS LTD

THIS EDITION PUBLISHED 2017

© 2017 UNIVERSAL STUDIOS.

1 3 5 7 9 10 8 6 4 2

CENTUM BOOKS LTD, 20 DEVON SQUARE, NEWTON ABBOT, DEVON, TQ12 2HR, UK
BOOKS@CENTUMBOOKSLTD.CO.UK

CENTUM BOOKS LIMITED REG. NO. 07641486

A CIP CATALOGUE RECORD FOR THIS BOOK IS AVAILABLE
FROM THE BRITISH LIBRARY

PRINTED IN CHINA

ILLUMINATION PRESENTS

DESPICABLE ME 3 ™

COMPLETE GUIDE TO
GADGETS AND VEHICLES
PLUS OTHER COOL STUFF!

Keep your eyes peeled for these letters hidden throughout the book. When you find one, note it down here and then unscramble the letters to make the name of one of the gadgets here.

→ JoakeThomas

B

centum

WELCOME TO A COMPLETE GUIDE TO GADGETS AND VEHICLES

PLUS other cool stuff!

Welcome, one and all, to the most comprehensive guide to gadgets ever compiled for the *Despicable Me* universe!

Do you know the best part of being a villain or a spy? Is it the fabulous outfits? Possibly. Is it the excitement? Well, that's good too, but by far the greatest things about being a villain or a spy are the GADGETS!

Not only is having a gadget in your hand an easy way to make you look super-cool, but they can help you escape from a tight spot!

I look super-cool without a gadget in my hand too.

You also need a bit of luck.

This book contains blueprints and details on all the coolest gadgets that Gru, Lucy and the villains have ever used, as well as some of the awesome locations.

So what are you waiting for? Read on and equip yourself with facts and stats on all the latest gadgets.

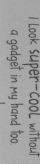

This book says it's the most comprehensive guide ever compiled, but did it include the first-hand experience of the greatest villain-turned-spy of all time? It did not! So keep an eye out for notes throughout the book by me, Gru, who has used and helped to create most of these gadgets.

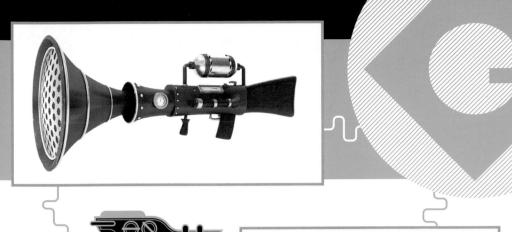

FART GUN

FREEZE RAY

FIRE BLASTER

BOOGIE ROBOT

FELONIUS GRU

Never in the history of villainy and espionage has a single person's career path been as back-and-forth from villain to spy . . . and back again as Gru's.

He is widely credited with pulling off both the greatest criminal heist ever when he shrunk and stole the moon, but also with saving the world from El Macho's PX-41 unstoppable Minion army.

Gru is also now a father and husband – so you might imagine there is never a dull moment in the Gru household. Let's learn more about him.

There is no proof that I did this. But also, after I did do this, I put it back!

I'm never credited for the time I was a legitimate business man – making delicious jams and jellies.

NAME:	Felonius Gru
OCCUPATION:	Villain (former)
	AVL spy
FAMILY:	Lucy Wilde (wife), Margo, Edith and Agnes (daughters), his mum, Dru (twin brother).
MOST LIKELY TO SAY:	"Assemble the Minions!"
OTHER ACHIEVEMENTS:	Children's book writer – 'One Big Unicorn'.
	Stole the Queen of England's crown from Scarlet Overkill's hands as a tween.

It's a **puppet book.**
My nose is the unicorn's
horn. Not to pat myself on
the back, but it's the best
book ever.

GRU'S ROCKET CAR

It's the must-have vehicle for any villain, spy or . . . family man.

Fully equipped with gadgets, rocket thrusters, there's not a safer car you could drive to commit the world's biggest crime, save the world or drive three girls to a ballet recital.

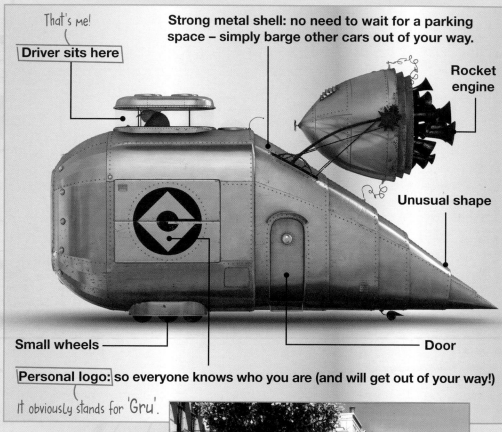

That's me!

Driver sits here

Strong metal shell: no need to wait for a parking space – simply barge other cars out of your way.

Rocket engine

Unusual shape

Small wheels

Door

Personal logo: so everyone knows who you are (and will get out of your way!)

It obviously stands for 'Gru'.

The perfect vehicle for an early morning coffee run.

Slim in width so it can fit through narrow spaces

Much taller than all other cars on the road

Except when it's been shrunk by a shrink ray.

Original blueprint for the rocket car.

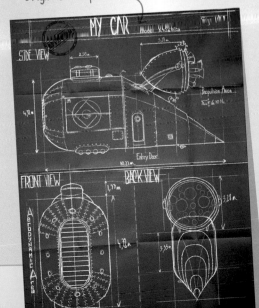

MY CAR Model 44.84 bcn

SIDE VIEW

Propulsion Area

Entry Door

FRONT VIEW   BACK VIEW

Aerodynamic Area

On the phone with my mum here.
That's why I look grumpy.

GRU'S HOUSE

This place is home to Gru and his family, as well as his Minions, and contains a secret lab underneath, which functions as a base for all operations and adventures.

Before Gru adopted the girls or married Lucy, this scary looking house was Gru's bachelor pad. It stands out from all the other white painted houses in the neighbourhood, with a dark and sinister colour scheme which says 'Stay away or else'.

When Margo, Agnes and Edith moved in, they made this their home too.

You can see their toys in the front garden, and chalk drawings on the drive.

We planted some flowers in the flowerbed here, so I always make sure Kyle goes POTTY in my neighbour's garden.

ENTRANCE TO GRU'S LAIR

There isn't really any cooler addition to any home than a secret entrance into a lair.

If you ever find yourself in Gru's house, here's a step-by-step guide to the secret entrance.

STEP 1: Walk into this room.

Button is HERE

Seat part of the chair moves to HERE.

STEP 2: Sit on the Rhino chair and press the red button on its left leg. Don't be alarmed, but the seat part of the chair will move into the centre of the room at some speed, so hold on.

STEP 3: Look up and you'll see that the cannon has moved above your head. It's going to come down over you.

STEP 4: |Don't be alarmed| at the cannon hurtling down towards you, but definitely keep your arms and legs close to you – the cannon becomes a glass tube.

STEP 5: Meanwhile, the room floor has been raised to reveal a coorot clcvalor. The tube is lifted backwards into the elevator.

STEP 6: The elevator descends into the lair.

~~GRU'S~~ LAIR

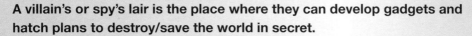

Whoever's Lair this is, they're obviously **very** cool and handsome.

A villain's or spy's lair is the place where they can develop gadgets and hatch plans to destroy/save the world in secret.

There's nothing that ruins a perfectly good plan more quickly than prying eyes snooping into what you're doing – so keeping the lair secret is top priority.

It's important for a lair to have space and functions to cover lots of different plans. Including:

EXACTLY! Please refer to my note on the previous page.

A big stage from which to deliver grand plans or pep talks to your employees/Minions.

Mission control for rocket launches.

A yoga studio – a relaxed mind is a productive mind!

A lab to create new gadgets.

ASSEMBLE THE MINIONS!

If you're looking for an army to help you go through and complete all your top-secret plans, then a Minion army is the only one you'll need.

Minions are unusual . . . creatures. If you've ever wondered what the anatomy of a Minion is like, then wonder no more and look at their blueprint below.

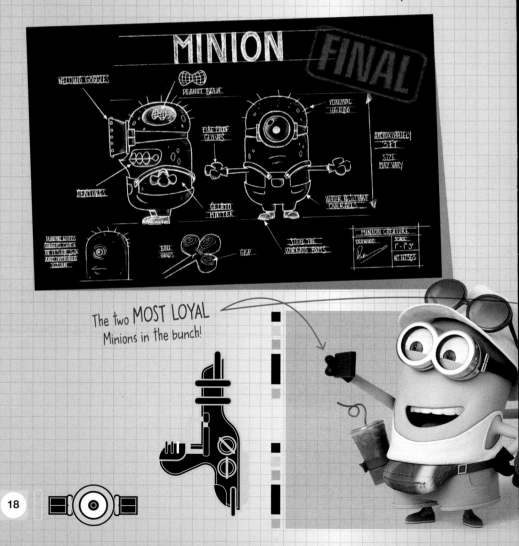

The two MOST LOYAL Minions in the bunch!

The Minions have all sorts of names, like Bob, Carl and Tim.

But others have other names too –
let's meet some of the army.

Mel

**You'll recognize Mel by his grumpy
face, one-eye and his distinct hair –
bald on top, hair around the sides!**

Mel leads the Minions revolt when they
decide that they miss being evil and they
want to find a new master with more
villainous ways.

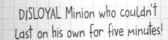

DISLOYAL Minion who couldn't
last on his own for five minutes!

Dave and Jerry

**These two often travel as a pair, but it's
easy to tell them apart. Jerry has spiky hair,
whereas Dave's is parted in the middle.**

They accompany Gru to Freedonia,
and spend a lot of time tormenting Dru's
butler with Edith.

FREEZE RAY

It's cooled down some **very hot** situations... It's particularly useful when you want to shorten a coffee shop line.

The Freeze Ray is one of Gru's favourite gadgets.

It was invented by Dr Nefario who first showcased it at Villain Con in 1968 – and first used soon afterwards during the mysterious disappearance of the Queen of England's crown.

A young boy's first heist in an extinguished career of villainy.

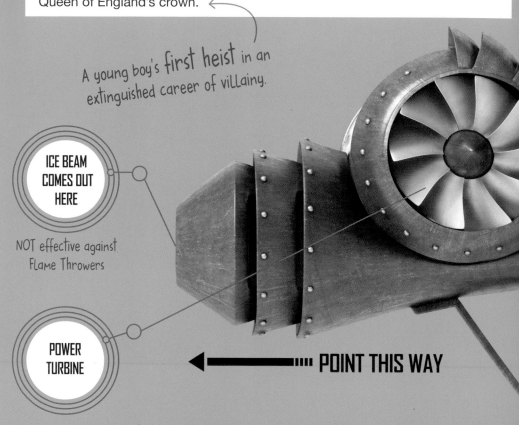

ICE BEAM COMES OUT HERE

NOT effective against Flame Throwers

POWER TURBINE

◄━━━━━ ⅢⅢ **POINT THIS WAY**

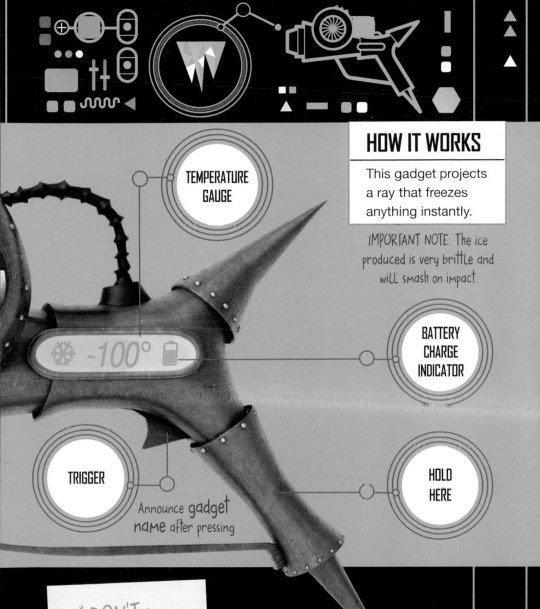

TEMPERATURE GAUGE

HOW IT WORKS

This gadget projects a ray that freezes anything instantly.

IMPORTANT NOTE: The ice produced is very brittle and will smash on impact.

BATTERY CHARGE INDICATOR

❄ -100° 🔋

TRIGGER

Announce gadget name after pressing

HOLD HERE

* DON'T leave unattended near the girls.

FIRST appears in DESPICABLE ME.

FART GUN

The idea of this hilarious, amazing and perhaps slightly pointless gadget was born from a simple mishearing.

Have you ever noticed how 'dart' sounds very similar to 'fart'? Well, from that, the Fart Gun was born, with the ability to seriously stink out a room.

Dr Nefario did use the Fart Gun to knock out a PX–41 EL Macho... The **stinkiest** defeat EVER!

A 21 Fart Gun salute is the **highest** honour.

Fart comes out here

Make sure you aren't downwind.

Pressure gauge   **Gas canister**

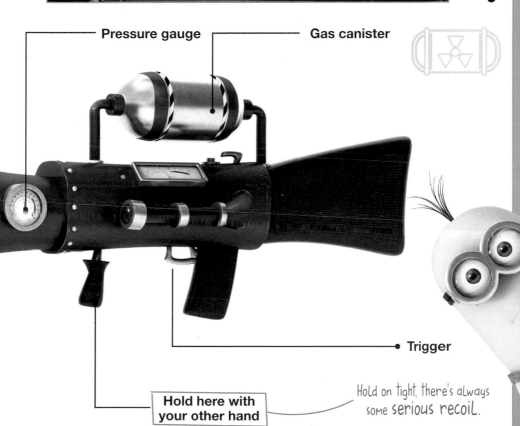

Trigger

Hold here with your other hand

Hold on tight, there's always some serious recoil.

COOKIE ROBOTS

A wise man, who was a little hard of hearing, once said that the ideas for the best gadgets are born from misunderstanding. From the same ears and brain that misheard and created the Fart Gun, came the Cookie Robots.

Oh wait, this isn't one of the gadgets that was misheard, that was Boogie Robots . . . it turns out to be an easy mistake to make.

These robots are disguised as cookies, and can be delivered into an unsuspecting home via a cookie box.

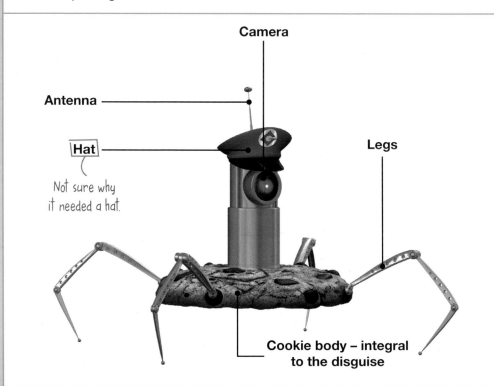

Camera

Antenna

Hat

Not sure why it needed a hat.

Legs

Cookie body – integral to the disguise

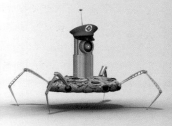

To learn all about Boogie Robots turn to page 46.

Stupid Vector, he had no idea these weren't **real** and **delicious** cookies!

MARGO, EDITH AND AGNES

They're the three little orphans who stole Gru's heart.

The sisters spent years dreaming of having loving parents, and now they have them – and a family that keeps getting bigger.

MARGO

Margo is the oldest and is going through a teenage phase – but she is still the responsible oldest sister who puts her family first.

When the family goes to Freedonia, Margo finds herself a little too involved in the culture . . .

Far too involved for my liking!

EDITH

When **Edith** meets her new Uncle Dru, she thinks it's great because he encourages all her most devious schemes. After spending time pranking Dru's butler, Fritz, she is quick to join Agnes on her unicorn quest – the money she'll get from selling a video of a unicorn would make her fabulously rich!

AGNES

Agnes has had two lifelong dreams – one was to be adopted into a loving family. CHECK! The second is to have a pet unicorn . . . and when she visits Freedonia she hears about a local legend that unicorns may be living in a nearby forest. How could she resist sneaking off on a quest to find a real unicorn?

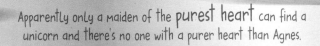

Apparently only a maiden of the **purest heart** can find a unicorn and there's no one with a purer heart than Agnes.

27

OPERATION:

RECLAIM THE SHRINK RAY FROM VECTOR

Gadgets are useful for many things and aren't just for looking cool. For instance, you can use them when doing some reconnaissance around the home of someone who has maliciously 'acquired' something of yours.

To read all about Vector, turn to page 34.

When Gru was trying to reclaim the Shrink Ray from Vector's vault, he got to test out a range of gadgets to try and get inside. Unfortunately for Gru, Vector's fortress was impenetrable.

GADGET 1: X-Ray vision goggles and ear trumpet
Great for looking through and listening through walls – so there are no surprises when you jump over.

Not so useful when there's a hidden boxing glove in the wall. Ouch.

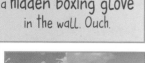

GADGET 2: Jet pack
Look super-cool as you smoothly and quickly glide through the air over walls and other structures.

NOTE: do not land on a hidden trap floor that can spring you back over the wall.

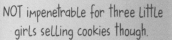

NOT impenetrable for three little girls selling cookies though.

GADGET 3: Grappling hooks and climbing gear
Climb up the side of tall buildings with ease!

This gadget is **easily defeated** by saws and other sharp objects.

GADGET 4: Subterranean gear
Perfect for sneaking in through the sewers. With light-sensitive goggles so you can see in the low-light, as well as tracking equipment to get you where you need to go.

Don't try this route if your nemesis has a pet **shark**.

Via the system that flushes away the waste from when you 'need to go'! Ha ha!

The most important thing though, when going on this sort of 'reclaiming' mission, is to do your research beforehand. So you don't end up in this situation:

SHRINK RAY

The SR-6, or Shrink Ray, was developed in a top-secret lab, until it was **stolen by Gru and his Minions . . .** and then stolen by Vector . . . and then stolen back by Gru. (Its location and 'ownership' history is complicated!)

SPARK POINTS COME OUT OF HERE WHEN ENGAGED AND SPIN AROUND UNTIL ENOUGH ENERGY IS GATHERED TO FIRE THE BEAM.

WHEN HOLDING EACH OF THESE HANDLES AND MOVING THEM INTO POSITION, THE SHRINK RAY WILL ACTIVATE.

BEAM COMES OUT OF HERE

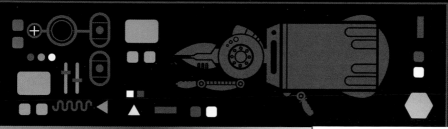

HOW IT WORKS

The Shrink Ray shrinks any object in its beam into a smaller version of itself.

THINGS KNOWN TO HAVE BEEN SHRUNK BY SR-6

Elephant
Minion
Gru's Rocket Ship
The moon
Vector's toilet

THE NEFARIO PRINCIPLE

While working in Gru's labs, Dr Nefario discovered that the shrunken state of an object is not permanent. In fact, he also discovered that the greater the mass of an object, the faster the shrunken object returns to its normal size.

Dr Nefario named this principle after himself . . . because who wouldn't name something they've discovered after themselves!

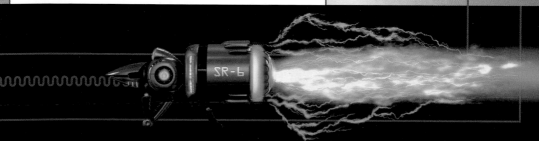

SR-6

PLANS TO STEAL THE MOON

It's often called the greatest crime of the century. Here are some exclusive blueprints from the planning of the famous heist.

Before you start any plan, it's important to weigh the pros and cons of the mission.

This isn't such an issue if, like me, you're **bald.**

GRU'S PLAN TO STEAL THE MOON
POTENTIAL RISKS & SIDE EFFECTS

HOPEFUL DESTRUCTION
* CIVILIZATION
* LIFE FORMS
* WEREWOLVES
* CHEESY ART

COLLATERAL DAMAGE
* NO ECLIPSES
* LACK OF NIGHT LIGHT
* NO HAIRDRESSER OPEN LATE

POSSIBLE BONUS EFFECTS
* TOTAL DARKNESS
* GOOD NIGHT SLEEP
* NO MORE BAD SONGS ABOUT THE MOON

PSYCHOLOGICAL EFFECTS
* CONFUSION
* DISORIENTATION
* PERPLEXITY
* SADNESS

SATISFACTORY POINTS
* OWNERSHIP
* BRAGGING
* PURE JOY

ENVIRONMENTAL EFFECTS
* BIRD MIGRATIONS
* TIDES
* NO MORE MOONLIGHT WALKS ON THE BEACH

GRU'S PLAN TO STEAL THE MOON
ROCKET

Plan and think about the tools that you'll need to successfully complete the mission – in this case, a rocket and the Shrink Ray. Also, think about how the plan would roughly work. This stage involves quite a few equations and sums.

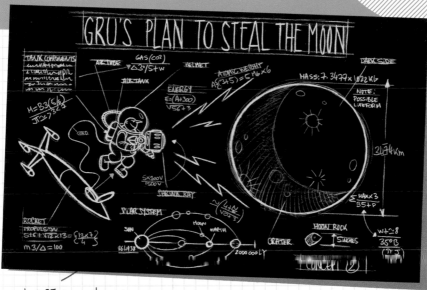

I'm NOT drawn to scale.

Finally, plan out in detail.

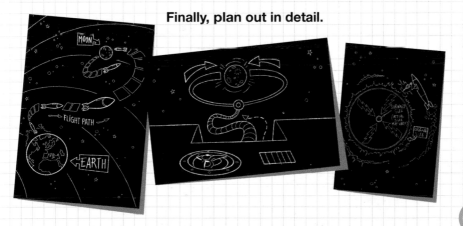

FACT FILE:

VECTOR

A 'vector' is a mathematical term. It's a quantity represented by an arrow with both direction and magnitude.

Let's learn all about the (former) world's greatest villain who adopted this as his name.

Vector or Victor, they're both nerd names.

REAL NAME:	Victor Perkins
GADGETS OWNED:	Piranha gun, Squid Launcher
VEHICLES:	Vector's Plane
LIVES:	In the Fortress of Vectortude
MOST RECOGNIZABLE FEATURE:	Orange jogging suit
BEST KNOWN FOR:	Stealing one of the Pyramids of Giza and replacing it with an inflatable replica
MOST LIKELY TO SAY:	"Hey, Gru! Try this on for . . . size?!" "Curse you, tiny toilet!"
FAVOURITE FLAVOUR OF COOKIES: Coconutties	

But really, they're pyjamas.

R

VECTOR'S GADGETS

It's all well and good to be called the world's greatest villain by pulling off a major crime, but you need to have other strings to your bow as well.

For most villains, they also invent their very own gadgets. Here are some of the gadgets Vector invented.

PIRANHA GUN

The perfect gun if you want a meat-hungry piranha to chase and bite your opponent. And the piranhas are always angry when they come out, and who wouldn't be, after being squashed into a gun and then fired out?

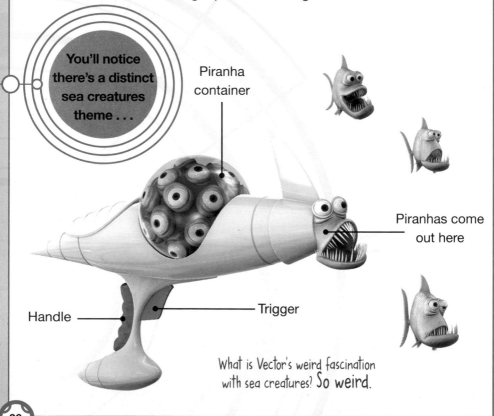

You'll notice there's a distinct sea creatures theme . . .

Piranha container

Piranhas come out here

Handle

Trigger

What is Vector's weird fascination with sea creatures? So weird.

SQUID LAUNCHER

The great thing about squids is that they have suckers on their tentacles, which is perfect if you want to hitch a ride on the outside of a rocket as it blasts into space.

This is the squid launcher in action.

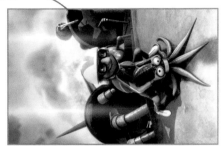

VECTOR'S SECURITY REMOTE

Vector can control all the security features for his fortress with this handy remote. Whether it's activating the punch glove features or unleashing his pet shark into the sewers – there's a button for everything.

GRU'S PLANE

A distinctive and awesome plane is an essential piece of kit for any aspiring super villain or spy.

You'll notice that Gru's plane has all the distinctive hallmarks of a Gru vehicle – the odd shape, silver colour and of course the 'G' logo – branding is key to any enterprise for a villain or a spy.

Every good plane starts out as a simple collection of ideas on a blueprint.

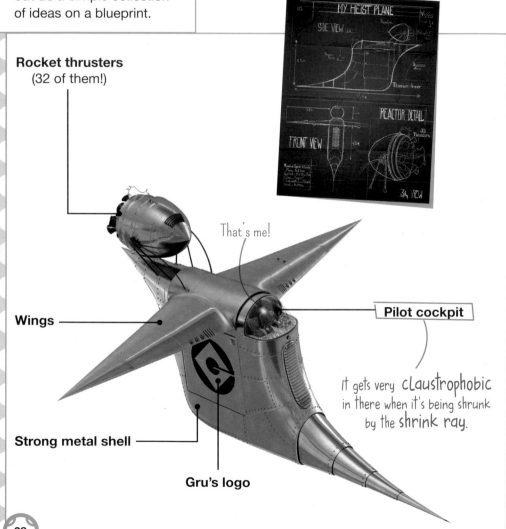

Rocket thrusters (32 of them!)

That's me!

Wings

Pilot cockpit

It gets very **claustrophobic** in there when it's being shrunk by the **shrink ray**.

Strong metal shell

Gru's logo

And if the plane ever did come under-attack from another unfriendly plane, it could defend itself like this:

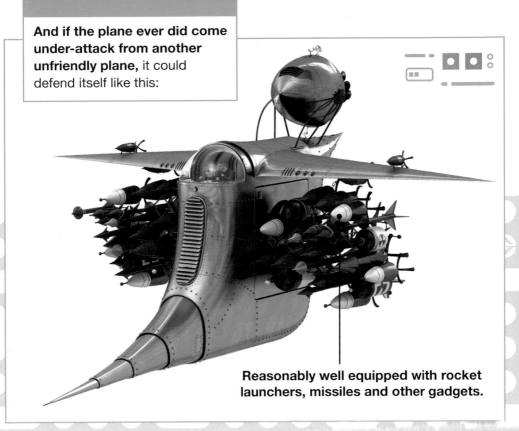

Reasonably well equipped with rocket launchers, missiles and other gadgets.

FACT FILE:

DR NEFARIO

Dr Nefario is Gru's gadget guru, as well as being his most loyal friend.

Dr Nefario has always considered Gru to be one of the greats of the supervillain world . . . and perhaps the spy world too.

REAL NAME: Joseph Albert Nefario

NOTABLE INVENTIONS:
Freeze Ray, Boogie Robots, Cookie Robots, Fart Gun, Rocket, Gru's car and plane.

SCIENTIFIC DISCOVERIES:
The Nefario principle

LESS NOTABLE INVENTIONS:
All-berry flavoured jam

Unfortunately, due to unknown circumstances, Dr. Nefario is currently frozen in carbonite. The Minions are currently trying to figure out a way to unfreeze him.

YOU CAN FIND OUT
MORE ABOUT THESE
GADGETS ELSEWHERE
IN THIS BOOK.

It's not known how old Dr
Nefario is . . . but it has been
suggested (although not
scientifically proven) that you can
tell how old someone is from the
size of their ears, since the ears
continue to grow throughout
someone's life. From the size of
Dr Nefario's ears, we can assume
that he's reasonably old.

This and the fact that he mishears
most things I say to him.

VECTOR'S PLANE

Every villain needs a personal brand that is recognised by all – and strikes fear into those who see it. For Vector, that's white and orange.

It's unusual shape, although it doesn't look very stable, is very useful for avoiding missiles.

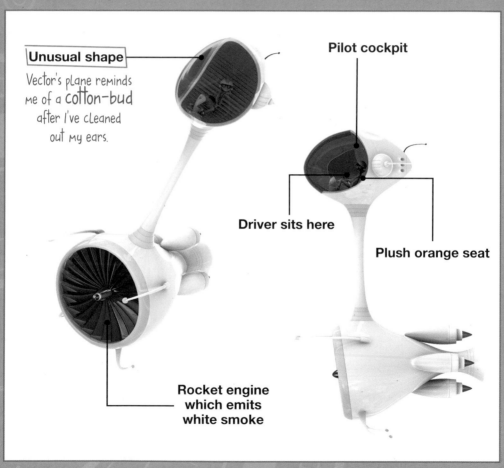

Unusual shape

Vector's plane reminds me of a cotton-bud after I've cleaned out my ears.

Pilot cockpit

Driver sits here

Plush orange seat

Rocket engine which emits white smoke

VECTOR'S SHIP

This airship is a hidden part of the dome of Vector's fortress –
Vector can activate it for a quick escape.

With the amount of **gadgets** and
vehicles Vector had, it's a good job his
dad was head of the Bank of Evil.

GRU'S ROCKET

When the Bank of Evil denied Gru any funding for his plan to steal the moon, the original plan for the rocket had to be scrapped.

Instead, a rocket was built from what Gru and his Minions could find.

STREAMLINE NOSE CONE

STRONG METAL SHELL

LOADS OF ROCKETS TO POWER THE ROCKET BEYOND EARTH'S ATMOSPHERE

THE COUNTDOWN TO BLAST OFF BEGINS

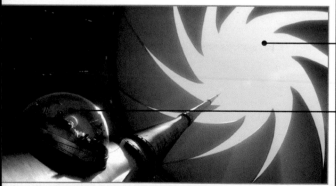

THE ROOF OPENING READY FOR THE ROCKET LAUNCH

GRU IN THE COCKPIT

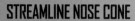

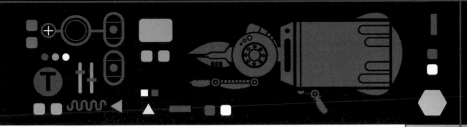

This rocket is what's known as a multi-stage rocket – it's essentially three rockets on top of each other. When one part has used all its fuel, it breaks away from the other parts, leaving the other parts to use their fuel.

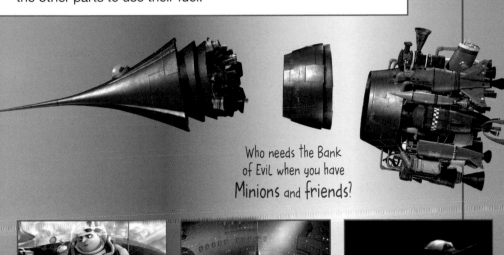

Who needs the Bank
of Evil when you have
Minions and **friends?**

BOOGIE ROBOTS

Born of a mishearing, but more importantly born to boogie – the Boogie Robots are exactly the sort of robots you'll want around when you want to jive around to music.

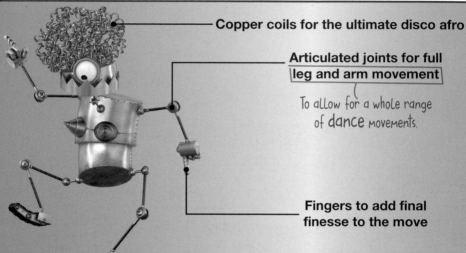

Copper coils for the ultimate disco afro

Articulated joints for full leg and arm movement

To allow for a whole range of dance movements.

Fingers to add final finesse to the move

I had no idea what I was looking at here.

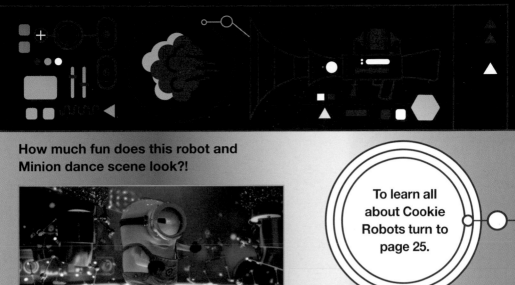

How much fun does this robot and Minion dance scene look?!

To learn all about Cookie Robots turn to page 25.

FACT FILE:

LUCY WILDE

Lucy has a happy home life with Gru and their three girls, as well as being partners with Gru at the AVL and an ever-expanding family – Lucy has everything she's ever wanted. Until she and Gru are suddenly fired...

NAME:	Agent Lucy Wilde
SPECIAL SPY SKILLS:	Breaking into places and surveillance
CURRENT STATUS:	Spy for AVL – unemployed
WEAPONS:	Flame thrower, Lipstick Zapper and Gadget Watch
TRANSPORT:	Multi-functional spy vehicle which transforms into a car, submarine and a plane
SPECIAL NOTES:	She is a master of combining different martial arts styles together. Also good at mimicking accents. Mother to three girls – Margo, Edith and Agnes

The name of this is always announced AFTER being fired.

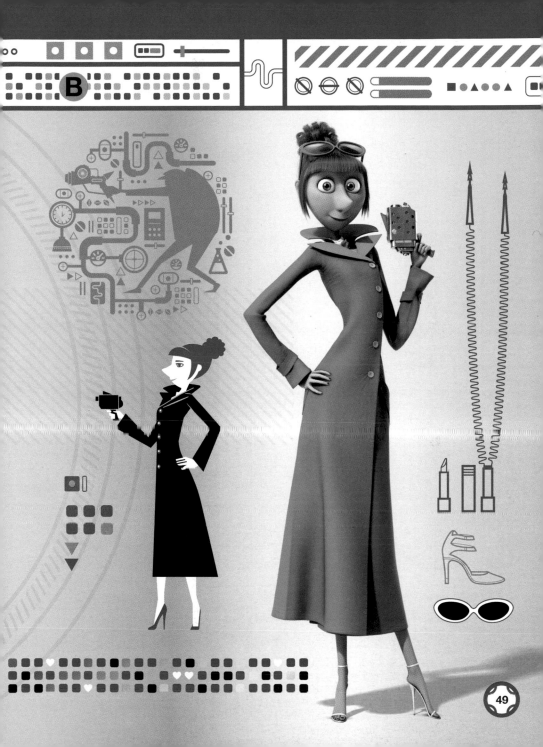

As with any spy's gadgets, Lucy's are discreetly hidden amongst objects she has about her person.

LIPSTICK ZAPPER

This is one of Lucy's favourite go-to gadgets. It fits in her handbag, and it is discreet up until the last minute, the intended target has no idea, until the very last second . . .

Looks like a real lipstick

Lucy gave this to me before she left for Australia.

Remove the lid and two prongs are thrown out towards intended target

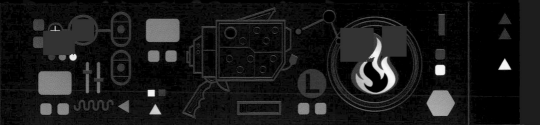

FIRE BLASTER

A husband and a wife are two opposite halves of a whole – and even before they met, Gru and Lucy had the opposite gadgets – fire and ice.

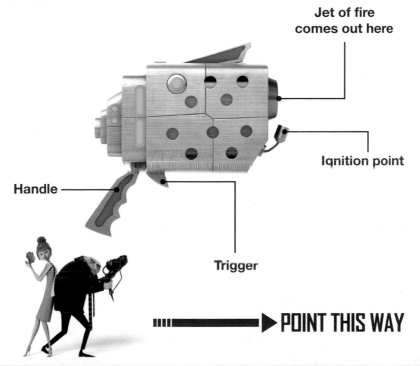

Jet of fire comes out here

Ignition point

Handle

Trigger

POINT THIS WAY

FIRST
appears in
DESPICABLE
ME2

LUCY'S SPY CAR

Every spy needs a way to get around – and this is the ultimate spy car.

If Lucy needs to travel around by land, water or air, then this vehicle can handle all situations.

CAR MODE

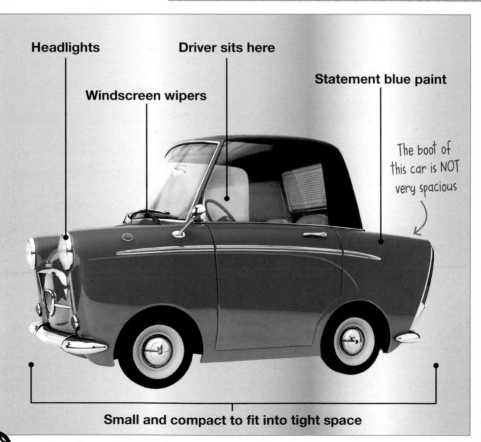

Headlights

Driver sits here

Statement blue paint

Windscreen wipers

The boot of this car is NOT very spacious

Small and compact to fit into tight space

SUBMARINE MODE

Headlights rise to here to light the way

Wings to stabilise

Propellers

There's also a **PLANE MODE** in case an air escape is needed.

53

AVL SUBMARINE

This submarine houses the secret Anti-Villain League Headquarters. As it's hidden underwater and constantly moving, its location is always unknown and can only be found by those who already know where it is.

Sleek design

AVL logo . . . so when you do find it, you know you've found the correct place

Black colour to camouflage in the shadows

A SNAPSHOT INSIDE THE SUBMARINE

It's not nice to be **kidnapped** and dragged into this place without being asked.

MAGNET AIRSHIP

This is the ship used to steal the PX-41 formula from the secret Siberian lab . . . well, technically it stole the entire lab.

Fittingly for a ship that looks like a giant magnet, it is actually a giant magnet.

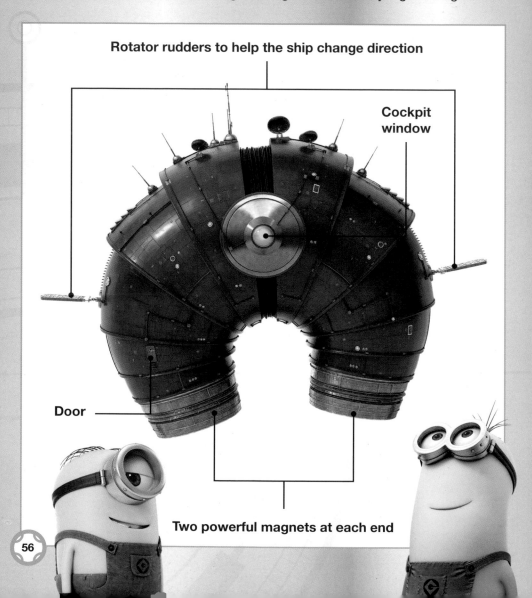

Rotator rudders to help the ship change direction

Cockpit window

Door

Two powerful magnets at each end

56

FIRST appears in DESPICABLE ME

GRAPPLING HOOK

This is perhaps the most versatile gadget in any spy's arsenal. It can be used to breach any wall or other obstacle which may find itself in a spy or villain's path.

This gadget is indispensable! There's always a wall to climb over.

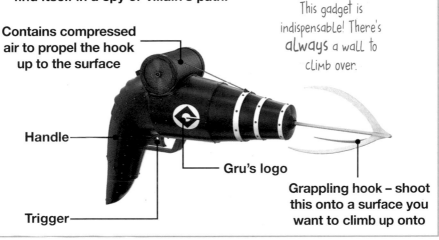

Contains compressed air to propel the hook up to the surface

Handle

Gru's logo

Trigger

Grappling hook – shoot this onto a surface you want to climb up onto

ROCKET LAUNCHER

For whenever you need a rocket launched somewhere, this is the perfect gadget.

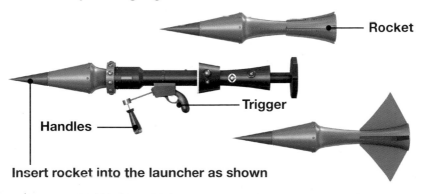

Rocket

Trigger

Handles

Insert rocket into the launcher as shown

FIRST
appears in
DESPICABLE
ME2

BAKE MY DAY!

When Gru went undercover in the mall to find out the whereabouts of PX-41, the AVL set him up in the bakery shop, 'Bake My Day'.

It might look like an ordinary bakery, but it's far from that.
There are hidden spy gadgets everywhere as well as delicious baked goods too!

cake stand

cupcake display fridge

The till doubles up as a secret spy computer.

coffee machine

entrance to the kitchen

BALLOON ANIMAL GUN

The perfect gadget for any fairy princess party. Especially if you need unicorn-shaped balloons.

I've had to hide this from Agnes, otherwise the house would be **filled** with unicorn balloons.

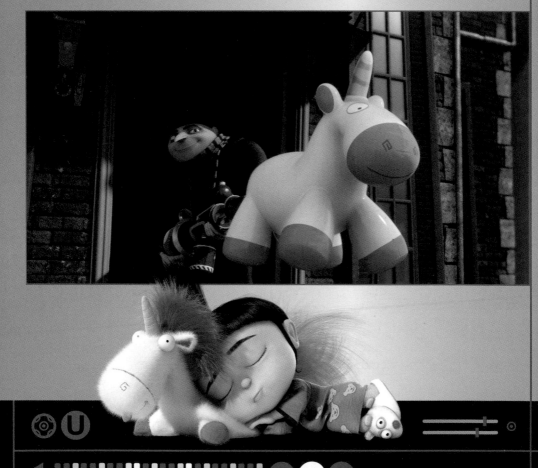

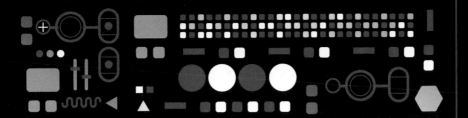

NANOBOT UNIVERSAL KEY

The microscopic particles in this key automatically arrange themselves when inserted into a lock, so it can unlock any lock known to man. Very useful when covertly sneaking into somewhere for information purposes…

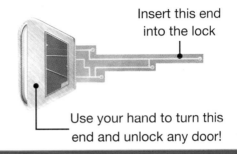

Insert this end into the lock

Use your hand to turn this end and unlock any door!

X-RAY GOGGLES

These are perfect to look through walls or to see what's inside a safe before you crack it open.

Do not look at another human with these on. It's an image you'll **never** erase from your memory.

SAFE CRACKER

Have you ever needed to crack a safe (when you've forgotten the code to your own safe, obviously)? Well, look no further than this gadget. Place it over the keypad or combination wheel and let it go to work.

FACT FILE:

EL MACHO

Mexican restaurant owner, passionate latin dancer, super-villain who stole PX-41 serum... He's a man of many talents, dressed in a cape and wrestling mask.

REAL NAME:	Eduardo Perez
REAL-LIFE OCCUPATION:	Owner of Salsa & Salsa Restaurant
TATTOOS:	Mexican flag across his chest
SUPER-VILLAIN NAME:	El Macho

NOTABLE EL MACHO LEGENDS:

He drinks snake's venom, then eats the glass it's served in.

He can headbutt an armoured truck with his head and then carry it away with his bare hands.

He faked his own death in the most macho way possible – riding a shark with two hundred and fifty pounds of dynamite strapped to his chest, into the mouth of an active volcano.

ALL that was left behind was a pile of singed chest hair.

EL MACHO'S LAIR

Every great villain and spy has a secret lair hidden somewhere. El Macho is no different – his lair is hidden in his large home on the top of a hill.

If you dance the correct tune on the correct tiles, then a door opens here to the lair.

Sometimes happy accidents in the correct order can open the door too – like guacamole falling out of a chip hat.

ICE CREAM TRUCK

If you ever fancy catching a Minion or two, there's one sure fire way to lure them into a trap – that's with ice cream, or as the Minions would say in Minionese 'GELATO'!

El Macho, with help from Dr Nefario, used the Minions' weaknesses for gelato to capture them all, luring them to the Ice Cream van before vacuuming them all inside with a giant ice cream cone.

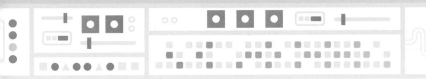

The Minions were then transported to a tropical island, so El Macho could inject them all with PX-41 serum to create an unstoppable Minion army!

THE GRUCYCLE

When you need to get somewhere in the nick of time and a rocket-powered car just won't do, the Grucycle is the vehicle for you.

EVERYONE must wear a helmet

Seats for two Minions

I look SO COOL and serious!

Pull these to brake

Handlebars

Pull these to brake

66

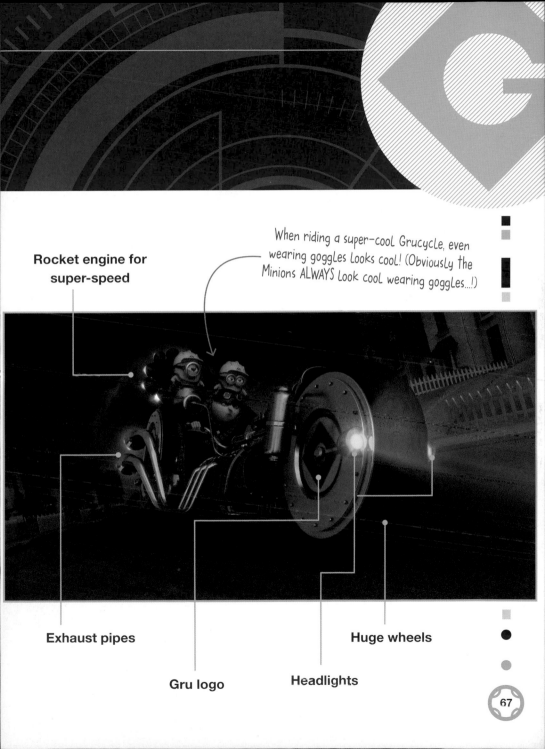

Rocket engine for super-speed

When riding a super-cool Grucycle, even wearing goggles looks cool! (Obviously the Minions ALWAYS look cool wearing goggles...!)

Exhaust pipes

Gru logo

Headlights

Huge wheels

PURPLE MINIONS A.K.A. EVIL MINIONS

Where the Minions are loveable, mischievous and yellow, the Evil Minions are dangerous, destructive and purple.

The Evil Minions are made to be an indestructible army. They are created by being injected with PX-41 serum, which mutates them.

When mutated, they are immune to many different weapons, including flame throwers and axes. They are also able to withstand the explosion of a bomb if they swallow it. Evil Minions will devour and destroy anything in their path.

To change Evil Minions back into Minions, you need to give them the antidote.

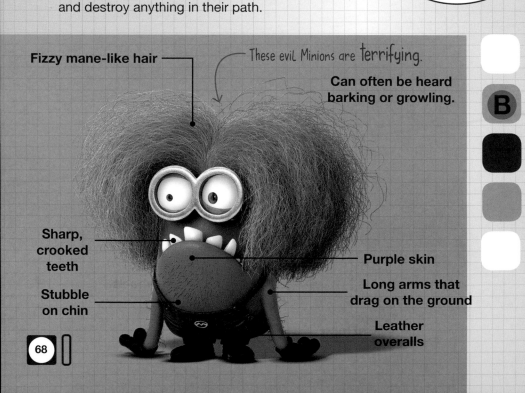

Fizzy mane-like hair

These evil Minions are terrifying.

Can often be heard barking or growling.

B

Sharp, crooked teeth

Purple skin

Stubble on chin

Long arms that drag on the ground

Leather overalls

So glad my **Legitimate** business developing a line of jams and jellies came in useful.

FACT FILE: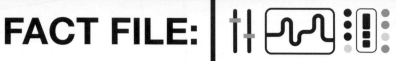

BALTHAZAR BRATT

He's the 80s TV star turned criminal mastermind.

When his TV show 'EVIL BRATT' was cancelled after he hit puberty, he vowed to seek revenge on the world that dared to cancel his show.

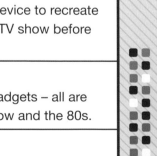

NAME:	Balthazar Bratt
GADGETS USED:	Self-Inflating Bubble Gum, Keytar, Disguises
VEHICLES:	Boat, Wingsuit, Wetsuit
OCCUPATION BEFORE VILLAINY:	Child TV Star
SIDEKICK:	Clive the Robot
EVIL PLAN:	To make a doomsday device to recreate the final episode of his TV show before it was cancelled.
OTHER ACHIEVEMENTS:	Bratt invents his own gadgets – all are inspired from his TV show and the 80s.
MOST LIKELY TO SAY:	"I've been a bad boy!" "Playing a villain on TV was fun – but being one in real life is better."

This guy's sense of style is **unbelievable.**
IT HURTS MY EYES.

DOODLE AN EPISODE OF 'EVIL BRATT'

If you were born in the 80s, you'll have been able to watch 'Evil Bratt', but if you weren't and since it isn't the 80s anymore (someone should let Bratt know this!), the next best thing is to create your own episode.

Doodle and write your episode on these pages.

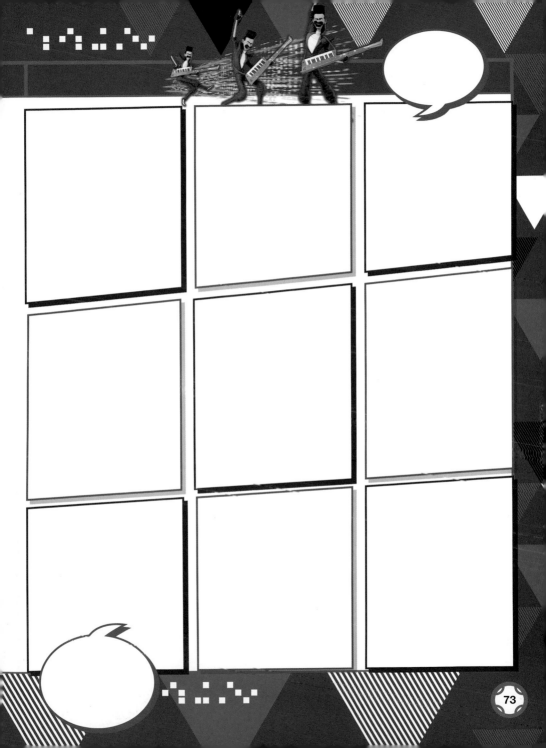

FACT FILE:

CLIVE THE ROBOT

Clive is Bratt's loyal sidekick.

He supports Bratt throughout all of his ideas, and is always ready to play an awesome 80s soundtrack.

> Minions make MUCH better sidekicks than robots.

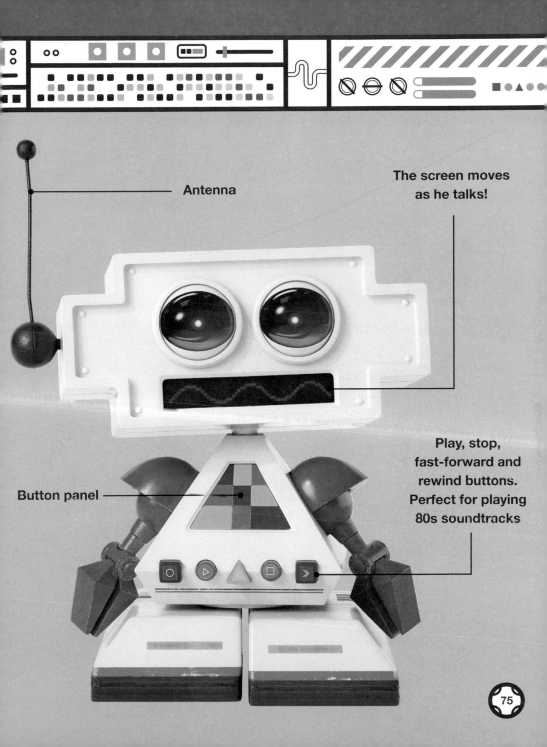

Antenna

The screen moves
as he talks!

Play, stop,
fast-forward and
rewind buttons.
Perfect for playing
80s soundtracks

Button panel

BRATT'S KEYTAR

It's the perfect gadget for an 80s aficionado –
part instrument, part sonic wave gadget.

Strap to hold the gadget in place

**Aux plug – plug it into
the speakers to make it
even louder!**

Powerful sound waves blast from this end ————

**Pressing these buttons changes the sound
to make some 80s synth sounds**

**Press these keys like a
keyboard to create a tune**

This gadget might look like JUST an instrument, but if you
get on the wrong end of the sound wave, it will literally
BLAST YOUR CLOTHES OFF.
(SO embarrassing!)

THE DUMONT DIAMOND AND BRATT'S PLAN

In order to exact his revenge, Bratt needs to build a Mega Diamond Laser, so he can carve out Hollywood and float it into space using bubble gum... just like he did during his favourite episode of 'Evil Bratt'.

Bratt has built the 'Mega Diamond Laser', but he needs the main piece – the perfect diamond.

The Dumont Diamond is the world's largest diamond.

It is cut in such a way that it focuses the laser, so it's powerful enough to cut out the whole of Hollywood.

As evil plans go, I'd give this a 2 out of 10.

FACT FILE:

MINI-SUBS

The perfect vehicle to stealthily chase someone at sea.

Agent 'Grucy', Dave and Jerry use these to follow Bratt to the sub.

I don't like this A LOT.

The window panel opens so the driver can get inside

Driver lies down in the tube

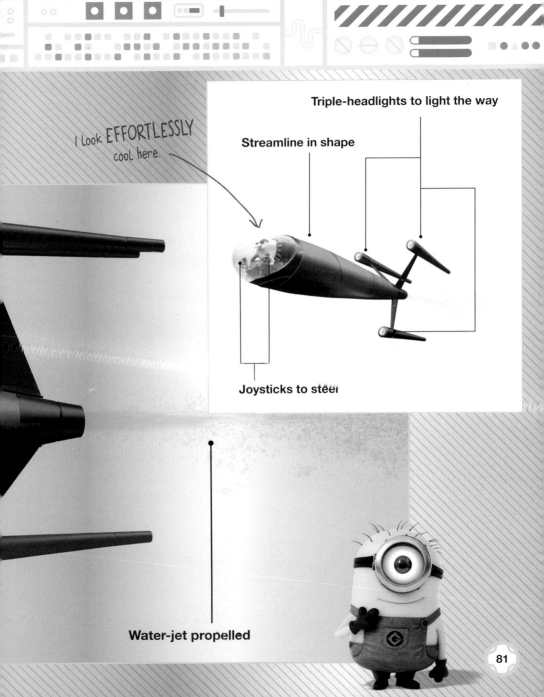

I look EFFORTLESSLY cool here.

Triple-headlights to light the way

Streamline in shape

Joysticks to steer

Water-jet propelled

DRU'S DAD'S VILLAIN SUITS

These outfits are perfect for when you're planning a heist . . . to say, steal back a diamond.

They have lots of modes, plus they're **super-stylish** . . . well, sort of!

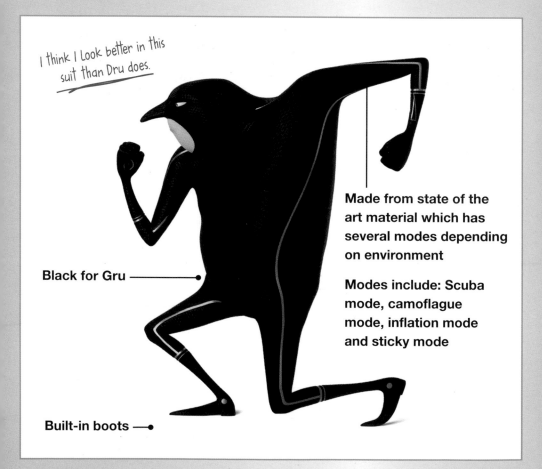

I think I Look better in this suit than Dru does.

Black for Gru

Built-in boots

Made from state of the art material which has several modes depending on environment

Modes include: Scuba mode, camoflague mode, inflation mode and sticky mode

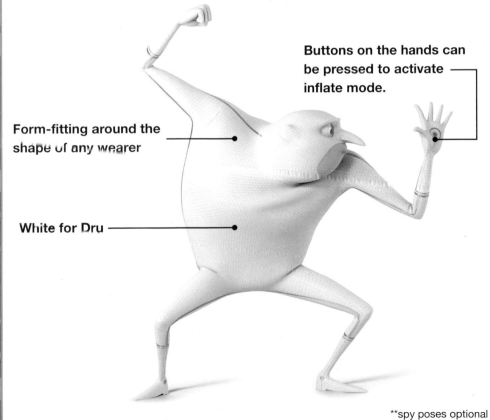

Buttons on the hands can
be pressed to activate —
inflate mode.

Form-fitting around the
shape of any wearer

White for Dru

**spy poses optional

FACT FILE:

DRU

Gru and Dru are identical twins, separated at birth.

Let's learn all about him.

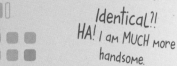

Identical?! HA! I am MUCH more handsome.

NAME:	Dru
OCCUPATION:	Most successful pig farmer in Freedonia
LIVES:	In the biggest mansion in Freedonia
HAIR COLOUR:	Blonde
GADGETS:	His dad's villain suits
TRANSPORT:	His dad's villain vehicle and a private jet
OTHER NOTES:	Dru is not an experienced villain, unlike his twin brother, Gru. He loves lollipops and was a big fan of the TV show, 'Evil Bratt'.

Hair is OVERRATED.

DRU'S VILLAIN CAR

FIRST appears in DESPICABLE ME3

When your dad's a super-villain, it means he will hand down his awesome gadgets and vehicles to you.

Winch

This car is totally AWESOME!

Sound system

The wheels turn to the side and inflate so it can travel in water

Two seats

Nose can turn into a drill to tunnel the way out of danger

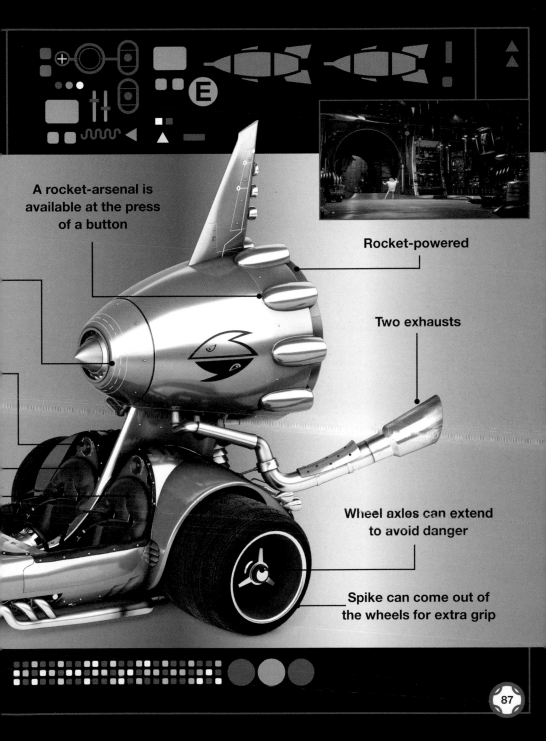

A rocket-arsenal is available at the press of a button

Rocket-powered

Two exhausts

Wheel axles can extend to avoid danger

Spike can come out of the wheels for extra grip

PIGS, PIGS, PIGS!

Dru owns the biggest pig farm in Freedonia.

Pigs might not be gadgets, but they are just as fun! And if you make friends with one, as Dave and Jerry did, you'll be able to ride around on them too.

At Dru's mansion, he has turned pig sculptures into the entrance to a secret lair! Lift up the statue-pig's head as shown and the entrance to the lair opens up below your feet.

Pig statue

Entrance to the lair appears here

Hidden lock

The entrance to my secret lair is better, but I admit this is PRETTY AWESOME TOO!

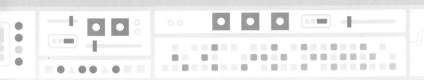

ears

eyes

snout

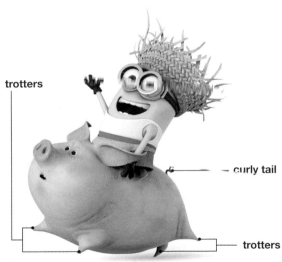

trotters

curly tail

trotters

**Minion riding the pig optional

MY SECRET LAIR

Every spy or villain needs a secret lair.

Design yours on these pages.

How will
you disguise
your entrance?
How will you
get in?

DOODLE YOUR OWN SIDEKICK

If it's always been your dream to have a robot sidekick, then this is for you! Doodle your sidekick below.

Don't forget to write about all the features it has, and what each button does.